Gospels

Nine Bible studies for students and young adult groups

by John Drane and Jim Belben

Jigsaw Series

Series editors: Jim Belben and Bruce Harris

Bible Society

BIBLE SOCIETY
Stonehill Green, Westlea, Swindon SN5 7DG, England

Cover photograph: © Sonia Halliday Photographs

First published 1990

British Library Cataloguing in Publication Data
Belben, Jim
   Gospels.
   1. Bible. N.T. Gospels – Critical studies
   I. Title   II. Drane, John W. (John William), *1946–*
   III. Series
   226'.06
   ISBN 0-564-07892-1

Photoset in Great Britain by The Castlefield Press Ltd and printed in Great Britain by Richard Clay Ltd, Bungay, Suffolk.

Bible Societies exist to provide resources for Bible distribution and use. Bible Society in England and Wales (BFBS) is a member of the United Bible Societies, an international partnership working in over 180 countries. Their common aim is to reach all people with the Bible, or some part of it, in a language they can understand and at a price they can afford. Parts of the Bible have now been translated into approximately 1,900 languages. Bible Societies aim to help every church at every point where it uses the Bible. You are invited to share in this work by your prayers and gifts. Bible Society in your country will be very happy to provide details of its activity.

CONTENTS

		Page
Introduction		5
How to use this book		6

Unit 1 A new look at Jesus

One	Foundations	9
Two	Horizons	15
Three	Take four	21

Unit 2 Four perspectives

Four	According to Mark	28
Five	According to Matthew	34
Six	According to Luke	39
Seven	According to John	46

Unit 3 Putting it together

| Eight | Past, present, and future | 51 |
| Nine | A matter of life and death | 56 |

Appendix	
Leader's notes	61
Summary of the steps for understanding the gospels	63
Other Jigsaw books	64

Introduction to the Jigsaw series

The diversity of the Bible

Many pieces . . .

The Bible is a vast library. Letters, poems and biography stand side-by-side with prayers, proverbs, and family trees. To confuse matters further, a single book, and sometimes a single passage, can contain many different styles. Finding your way about can be a very difficult business. So it is no surprise that many readers steer clear of all but the most popular books.

First and foremost, this series aims to set out a simple method for helping you understand any material you find in the Bible; to help you explore the unfamiliar books; to help you understand and apply what you find.

All the Bible is relevant. Although not all passages are directly applicable to you now, all were directly relevant to someone at some time. Discovering what God was saying to the original hearers is one key to understanding what God, through the Holy Spirit, is saying to you now.

Through this series you can discover an original approach to reading law, history, poetry, and prophets in the Old Testament; gospels and letters in the New Testament. You can refer back to this method in years to come – and use this as a valuable reference book.

. . . One picture

One factor holds all the diverse contents of the Bible together – it is about how God reveals himself to ordinary people. Although it is written by human writers, God's Spirit initiates and controls. God still speaks to us through its pages – thus we can refer to it as the "Word of God".

Of course, a method is not enough on its own. Many questions will be raised which cannot be answered simply. You will need to explore further on your own. But this method can help you cope with obscure material. Whether you are used to studying the Bible or not, this book will, I hope, open up new ideas and possibilities. It can help you think in the broadest terms – "What is God saying to me in this passage?"

How to use this book

The most important feature of this book is the nine steps for understanding the gospels, introduced session by session, and gathered for easy reference on page 64. This step-by-step approach means that you should tackle the sessions in the order they appear, because each session assumes some familiarity with the previous ones.

Maximum benefit will be obtained by doing all nine sessions over a nine-week stretch. The sessions are designed to be easy to lead and to let everyone participate. You don't need to have any previous knowledge of the passages you are studying, though it will always help if you have read them through beforehand. It will help if someone who has led groups before leads the first two or three sessions and then we suggest that a different person leads each subsequent session. There are notes to help in leading on page 61, which the leader will need to look at.

The time needed for each session will vary between one and one-and-a-half hours. Each session has a short starter to help break the ice and get into the subject matter. The bulk of each session consists of Bible study /application with rough timings given for each activity to help you plan. The On your own sections at the end of each session introduces material to help prepare for the following session, so it is important that it is done before the group's next meeting.

A good size for the group is from five to eleven people. Each group member will need a copy of this book, a copy of the Bible, and a pencil, rubber, and note-paper.

The gospels

Most of us have had a regular dosage of the gospels since childhood. We've been brought up on a diet of Christmas stories, miracles, parables, and much more. We recall one survey that suggested the British population in general was more familiar with the gospel than any other story bar Robin Hood.

But familiarity breeds contempt. Or so the saying goes. And there's plenty of evidence in our world to convince us that most people don't take a blind bit of notice of Jesus.

And sadly it's true that we can't recapture the sense of wonder and awe with which the early gospel stories were remembered, repeated, and treasured by the first Christians. Two thousand years of "progress" has seen to that. But let's set our sights a little lower: to take a fresh look; to learn from the stories, the comments, the teachings, and the attitudes of Jesus; and to try to take what we find out into the world with us.

In Unit 1 of this study booklet we will be establishing a new way of looking at Jesus through a series of nine steps for understanding the gospels. Unit 2 looks at the distinctives of each gospel. Unit 3 concludes by examining the overall impact of Jesus – in particular his teachings about the Kingdom of God and the significance of his death and resurrection.

Obviously, we can only cover small parts of the gospels in nine sessions. We have had to be selective in choosing particular stories and incidents. But those dealt with here are meant to be representative. They should help you to study other passages on your own, and ask similar questions about them.

Foundations

Aims

- ■ To decide what kind of document a gospel is

- ■ To see how the gospels reflect the concerns of the New Testament church

- ■ To see how the death and resurrection of Jesus are the focus of all four gospels

Starter

20 MINS

★ Imagine you have been commissioned to write the life story of a person from either the past or present. Choose someone you know something about.

On your own, set out on a piece of paper an outline of how you would organize their story. What periods or topics would you cover? Show where your book would start and end. What other events would you write about?

Now join up with three others and compare notes.

★ Then back together, discuss:

⟹ **What are the hallmarks of a good life story?**
⟹ **How is a biography different from a history book?**

★ What kind of document is a gospel? From what you already know about the gospels would you say they are life stories of Jesus, history books, or something else entirely?

Discuss your ideas about this briefly, then on your own, read our comment below.

Comment

❝ Although the gospels have superficial similarities to modern biographies or history books, the differences are perhaps more striking.

Modern history and modern biography are very concerned with 'chronological sequence'. The gospels, on the other hand, while they appear to tell a life story are not attempting a chronological reconstruction. It's no use asking whether one gospel got the story 'in the right order', and another 'in the wrong order'. They were not attempting the sort of sequencing we associate with historical writing.

History is there in the gospels. In Luke's gospel, for example, the historical context is described with great care. But it is always as background to the overriding concern which is with Jesus, and especially the last week of his life and his subsequent resurrection.

A modern biographer feels duty bound to research and tell most of a subject's life, while Mark, for example, (which has been called a passion narrative with a preface) starts his story with Jesus aged thirty, and devotes almost half of his gospel to the last week of Jesus' life. **"**

★ Now record your own provisional definition of a gospel below. You will have opportunity to change it later.

Tell your definition to the rest of the group. Note any common factors in the various definitions, then discuss:

⟳ **What do you expect to find out from your study of the gospels?**

Bible study

25 MINS

A. "That you may believe . . ."

★ Your group leader will have outlined the shape of this Bible study course. Hopefully it will meet some of your expectations, and also challenge you to new ways of thinking about Jesus and the gospels.

Our studies will introduce a series of steps for understanding and applying gospel writing in general. Not all of these are relevant all the time but they are important factors to consider when reading any section of the gospels. Nine key questions will be introduced over the first three sessions and these will be referred to in subsequent sessions. You will see they have been listed together for easy reference on page 64. The first of these is:

Step one

Identify the aim(s) of the gospel writers

We have already begun to tackle this step by comparing a gospel with other types of writing. If the gospel writers weren't aiming to create biography or history as we know it, what were they aiming for? We shall also be returning to the question many times throughout our studies of the gospel – and we'll find the answer is a bit like an onion – there's always another layer inside. And the deeper we go, the more we will understand about the aims of the gospel writers – and maybe they'll bring a tear to our eyes as well.

★ In this session we'll look at one of the most obvious ways of identifying the aims of the gospel writers. What do they say themselves about their aims?
Two of the gospel writers declare their aims very prominently.
Two people read out Luke 1.1-4 and John 20.30-31, and together list what the passages tell us about their aims.
John says he writes that we may believe that Jesus is the Messiah – and that could stand as a very adequate summary of the overall aim of all the gospel writers.
It is an "evangelistic" aim that informs every incident, every chapter, verse, and sentence of the gospels.

★ How do the writers help us to believe?
In three smaller groups read through the following passages. They will probably be so familiar to you that they will need no introduction. For the first Christians the death and resurrection of Jesus was the absolute centre of their faith. Their preaching and teaching revolved around it.

■ Group 1: Matthew 27.45-56
■ Group 2: Matthew 27.57-66; 28.11-15
■ Group 3: Matthew 28.1-10, 16-20

Each group identify what you think the writer wants his readers to believe (what details does he emphasize?), and how he is helping them to believe – or to put it another way, what barriers to belief is he helping them to overcome?
Read quickly through the following comment, then discuss:

⇨ **Which parts of this do you find it easiest to believe?**
⇨ **Which are hardest?**

Comment

❝ Matthew wants his readers to see that the death of Jesus was a cosmic event, with immediate cosmic consequences. An earthquake, the curtain of the temple torn in two, the resurrection of some who had died, all prove this. The death was more a victory than a defeat.

He also wants to make absolutely clear that Jesus really did die and really did rise to life again. So he dwells on the actualities of the death – who took the body, and where he put it; how closely the grave was guarded – and how impossible it was that the 'grave robber' thesis could explain away Christ's resurrection.

Finally, he wants his readers to know that the work the New Testament church was engaged in was given by the very instruction of Jesus himself. It was not an invention of the disciples.

Even some of the disciples in the very presence of Jesus himself had their doubts (Matthew 28.17), but they still worshipped. It is an invitation to the doubters to embrace faith in Jesus, as well as those who find it easy to believe. ❞

B. "How can I understand . . ."

★ On your own, read through the background material below.

Background

For us the gospel has become a book, but the word means simply Good News – or the message within the book. Jesus' impact during his lifetime was oral and personal. It was dynamic. People who met him or heard him could never forget him. And they passed on the stories of his exploits in a continuing "oral tradition". When Jesus presented the Good News he probably did not have in mind that what he did and said would become a book.

But the books were not long in coming. Only a few years after Jesus' death, his teaching was making its biggest impact not among those who had known him in Galilee, but in towns and cities many hundreds of miles away across the Mediterranean Sea. Even Rome itself had a strong and growing Christian community only fifteen years after the resurrection.

At first these people could learn about Jesus from the disciples, some of whom travelled extensively spreading the oral tradition very widely. But this had its drawbacks. The disciples could not be in all places at once, and in any case any self-respecting religious cause in the Roman world had to have a book to explain its teachings. So the gospels gradually came into existence – organizing and recording the oral tradition, to make it easier to put Jesus and his teachings to those whom the church was trying to teach.

★ The gospels are therefore not only the power behind the New Testament church, they are also the product of the New Testament church. Thus step 2 for understanding and applying gospels is:

Step 2

Relate the passage to the situation of the New Testament church

What was the situation of the New Testament church? For the rest of this session we examine a few of their distinctive concerns. What questions might be on the lips of the leaders of the first Christian churches? How about:

■ How do we explain Jesus to complete newcomers?
■ How can we sort out the chaos of our meetings?
■ How can we encourage believers facing difficult situations or persecution?
■ How can new believers grow into mature ones?
■ How do we resolve the knotty problems that threaten to tear the church apart?
■ How do we help believers to share the essentials of their faith with others?

(If this list sounds quite modern it should come as no surprise! But more of that later . . .)

★ Get into pairs. Each pair choose one of the following passages: Acts 8.26-40, 1 Corinthians 1.17-25, Acts 15.1-11, Acts 7.54–8.3, 1 Corinthians 11.17-22, Romans 13.1-7.

Summarize the situation that the early Christians found themselves in according to this passage, and compare with the list above. You may need to read between the lines a bit and imagine questions or conflicts that are implied by the passage.

You have been requested by church leaders to compile a dossier of facts, incidents, and memories about Jesus from the gospels, which can help in this situation. Writing takes time and parchment is expensive so you are limited to three passages, but you may wish to choose only one.

What aspects of, and what passages from, the gospels would be most useful in this situation? Do the leaders perhaps need one set of passages and the "ordinary" Christians another set?

★ Get back together. Summarize your dossiers, and discuss:

> ⟶ **Did you find what you needed in the gospels?**
> ⟶ **If not, what else did you want?**
> ⟶ **Do any silences in the gospels surprise you?**

Application

10 MINS

Finally, on the pieces of card provided, write:

1. Some aspects of your personal situation that you hope the gospels will speak to.
2. Some aspects of your church situation that you hope the gospels will speak to.

These are going to be discussed at a later session so don't put anything too personal unless you are prepared to talk about it with the group.

Briefly share anything that you've written on your cards. Those that have identified similar concerns, get together and pray for one another.

On your own

★ This session has required us to select passages from all over the gospels. A much better foundation for study is to read an entire gospel at one sitting. Sometime before the next session, speed read Mark's gospel. It shouldn't take more than ninety minutes.

It will be particularly useful preparation for the next session if, as you read, you note down all the places that Mark says Jesus visited.

2 Horizons

Aims

■ To see the gospels in their first century context

■ To see how Jesus and the gospel writers used the Old Testament

■ To investigate the stories surrounding Jesus' birth

Starter

20 MINS

★ On the next page is a simplified map of Palestine in the time of Jesus. Join with a partner and quickly plot on the map the route that Jesus took in his journeys around the country. Use Mark's gospel. Draw any journeys you are really sure about in pen; any that are more tentative in pencil.

⟡ **Does there appear to have been a turning point in Jesus' journey?**

⟡ **Where did Jesus spend most of his time?**

⟡ **Does anything about Jesus' movements surprise you?**

★ In session one we identified the gospels overriding concern with the last week of Jesus' life. In each gospel, however, the rest of Jesus' life is also divided into significant phases.

This, for instance, is how Mark is organized:

■ A prologue 1.1-8

■ The baptism and temptation of Jesus 1.9-13

■ Jesus' public ministry in Galilee 1.14– 9.50

■ From Galilee to Jerusalem 10.1-52

■ The last week in and near Jerusalem 11.1– 16.8
(including the report of the resurrection of Jesus 16.1-8)

■ The appearances and ascension of the risen Lord 16.9-20

On your map of Jesus' journeys, mark in a different colour each of these different phases of Jesus' life.

★ Each of the four gospels follow much the same pattern. Step 3 for understanding gospels is therefore:

Step three

> **Identify where this passage fits in the gospel story as a whole**

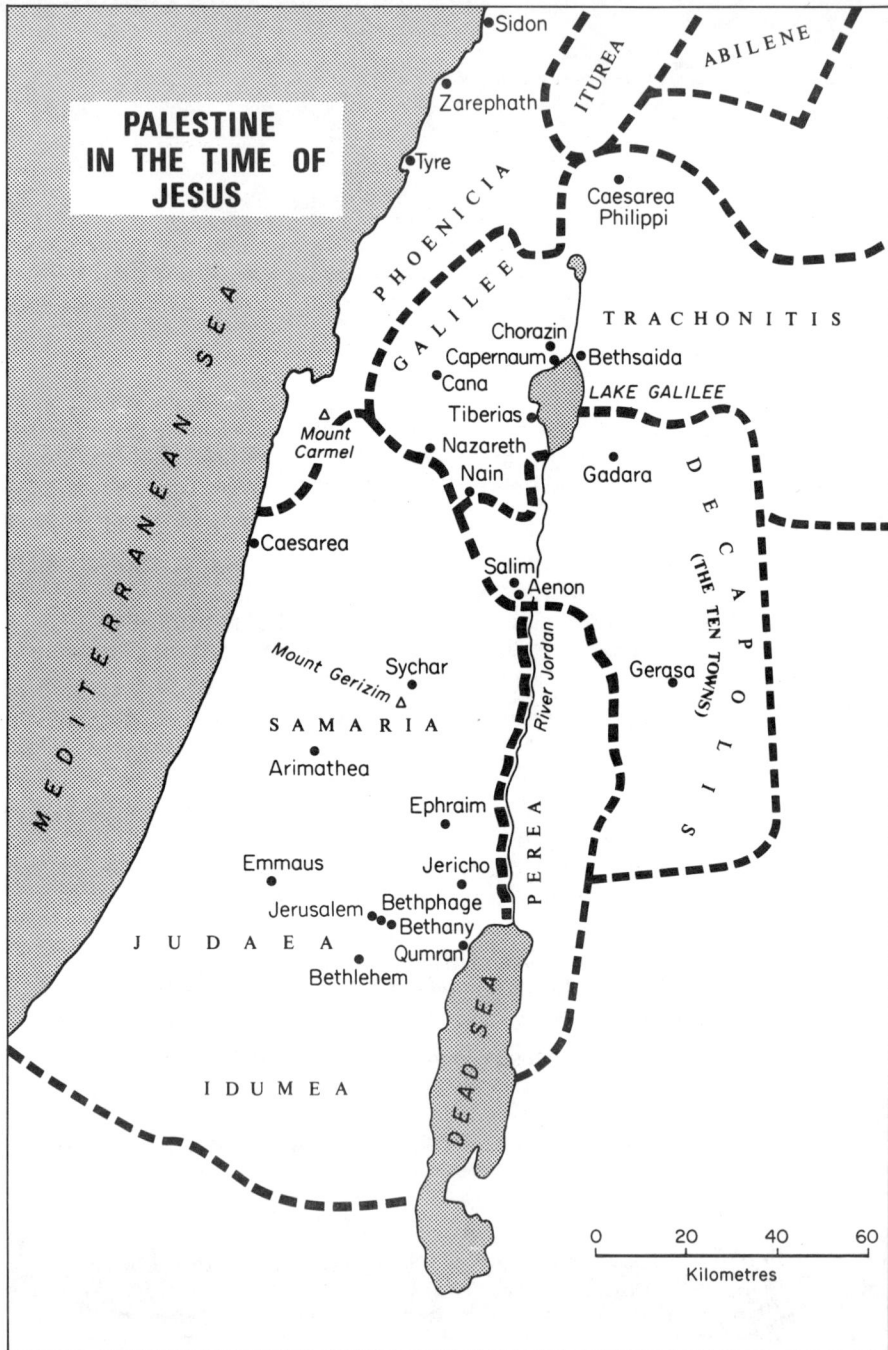

PALESTINE IN THE TIME OF JESUS

MEDITERRANEAN SEA

- Sidon
- Zarephath
- Tyre

PHOENICIA

ITUREA

ABILENE

- Caesarea Philippi

GALILEE

TRACHONITIS

- Chorazin
- Capernaum
- Bethsaida
- Cana

LAKE GALILEE

- Tiberias

△ Mount Carmel

- Nazareth
- Nain
- Gadara

DECAPOLIS (THE TEN TOWNS)

- Caesarea

- Salim
- Aenon

River Jordan

Mount Gerizim △

- Sychar
- Gerasa

SAMARIA

- Arimathea

- Ephraim

PEREA

- Emmaus
- Jericho
- Jerusalem
- Bethphage
- Bethany
- Qumran

JUDAEA

- Bethlehem

DEAD SEA

IDUMEA

0   20   40   60
Kilometres

We won't dwell on this as it's a very straightforward exercise, but it is nonetheless useful. In the different phases of his ministry the writers show Jesus was dealing with different people and different problems. He even teaches about different things. His public ministry in Galilee was characteristically filled with teaching about discipleship, while his last week in Jerusalem, on the other hand, includes teachings about the "end times" and debates with the authorities. Where the writer places a particular story, i.e. in what phase of Jesus' life, is one key to unlocking the meaning and significance of that passage for understanding Jesus. Sessions 2–9 take you through each of these phases in order:

- Session 2   Prologue
- Session 3   Baptism and temptation
- Session 4   Public ministry in Galilee
- Session 5 and 6   Galilee to Jerusalem
- Session 7, 8, and 9   The last week
- Session 9   Resurrection

Bible study

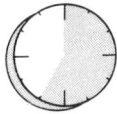

35 MINS

A. Jesus of Nazareth

★ Jesus of Nazareth? The name has a ring to it now. But in its time it might have been no more exotic than Bob of Birmingham, or Peter of Perth. Yet as a name it serves a purpose. It roots Jesus firmly in Palestine, in a small outpost of the vast Roman empire, a rugged area of a country that would hardly figure on a first century Mediterranean map. If you were searching for God it's not the first place, say, an educated Roman would think of looking.

But this was the world that Jesus found himself born into. What was so special about Palestine at that time? Why did God choose there, and why did he choose them? In answering these questions we will be using step 4 for understanding gospels:

Step four

Locate the events in first century Palestine

★ To get a sense of what Palestine was like in the first century there's really no substitute for a visit to Israel, though there are many good Bible handbooks available. Many things there are still as they were in Jesus' time. We expect your funds are as limited as ours, however, so your leader has done the next best thing to taking you to Galilee by bringing a bit of first century Galilee to you.

What does your piece of "Galilean archaeology" reveal to you about the political, economic, social, cultural, religious, or physical context of first century Palestine? Record your suggestions on a large piece of paper. If you are familiar with "spider diagrams" use one here.

★ Now let's see how that background surfaces in the stories of Jesus' birth that form the prologues to Matthew's and Luke's gospels. Split into two groups – one group read Matthew 1.18–2.23, the other read Luke 1.26-38 and 2.1-38.

Use your map to locate the events geographically. What other elements of the political, economic, social, religious, cultural and physical background you've identified above, surface in the story?

Come back together again, and show the others your conclusions.

★ This awareness of first century Palestine will be useful through the rest of this course. It will help provide a backdrop against which to view the events of Jesus' life. On a few occasions, when the cultural background suddenly seems to step forward and take a major part on the stage, it will help us realize what is going on.

Finally, it should help us keep in mind that Jesus' life was lived in a world with very different realities and beliefs from ours – a land of olive trees and vineyards, of shepherds and fishermen, where medicine would have no answer to some of the simplest diseases; where scientific explanation was unimportant and religious rituals and concepts framed almost everybody's lives.

★ Now together as a group, go back and consider steps 1–2 which were introduced in session 1. Apply step 1 to the Christmas story as a whole – Matthew and Luke's versions taken together. For step 2, focus on the stories of the wise men (Matthew 2.1-12) and the shepherds (Luke 2.8-20). We'll be returning to these stories at the end of the session, but are there any brief comments before we move on?

B. "As the prophet wrote ..."

★ Step 5 for understanding gospels is:

Step five

Identify the Old Testament background to the passage

You will already have begun to do this in the earlier activity, but it's useful to focus more closely on it. Remind yourself quickly of how Old Testament background surfaced in the two passages you studied earlier, by reading the following comment.

Comment

" Both Matthew and Luke draw attention to Jesus' family line back to David, (although Luke leaves his genealogy of Jesus for a later chapter). David, the king of Israel in its golden age before civil war and external aggression ripped the nation apart, was one of the popular models for the Messiah.

Luke also focuses on how Mary and Joseph acted in accordance with the Old Testament laws concerning circumcision and sacrifice.

Matthew characteristically quotes from the Old Testament to show how Jesus' birth is fulfilling prophecy (1.23, 2.6, 2.18). Luke, also typically, records both Mary's and Simeon's songs of praise, which are liberally sprinkled with the thoughts and phrases of the Old Testament.

Matthew's protagonists all hear from God through dreams – very much an Old Testament tradition. **"**

★ There is certainly nothing unexpected about the widespread use of Old Testament material in the gospels. The Old Testament was as much part of the lives of Jesus' followers as the gospels are part of ours. In those days, long before personal organizers did away with the need to remember anything, people would commit Scripture – the Law, the Psalms, the Prophets – to memory. Their minds were swimming with "OT Fax" which surfaced throughout the gospels. How Jesus and the gospel writers used the Old Testament can give us deeper insight into the meaning they attached to Jesus' life.

Each of you will be given a piece of "OT Fax" which surfaces in the New Testament. From memory or common sense alone, try to establish where in the New Testament they are used. They are all in the gospels, and all four gospels are represented.

You might do this in two stages. Start with speculating what kind of event in Jesus' life you might expect this to relate to; then find the incident in the gospels to see if you are right. It isn't a contest, so do help each other.

★ When most of the passages have been identified, discuss briefly:

> ▷ **How do you think the original readers would respond to the inclusion of Old Testament material in the gospels?**

★ The final part of this session will return to the story of the incarnation. Can you find a fresh way of communicating the Christmas story today? To make it more difficult, let's see if you can find a fresh way of communicating the Christmas story through the most hackneyed medium of the lot – the Christmas card.

The task is to design a new and meaningful Christmas card. In pairs, choose who your Christmas card is for – it could be someone you both know, someone famous, or someone fictitious. Identify some elements from Matthew or Luke's stories that you wish to use, and decide on an illustration and greeting for your card.

On your own

★ Some time before the next session read through the only story we are given about Jesus' childhood – Jesus in the Temple at Jerusalem. It's in Luke 2.41-52, but read verses 39-40 as well for context.

Use steps 1, 3, and 4 to establish some background. Then in anticipation of session 3, try out step 6.

Ask what the writer wants to emphasize

In particular, what do you think the writer wants to emphasize about Jesus by the following: that Jesus and his parents were going to the Passover in Jerusalem; that he was missing for three days; that the Jewish teachers were amazed at him?

Take four

Aims

- To discover the problems and strengths in having four gospels
- To ask what the writers want to emphasize about Jesus
- To learn from Jesus' baptism and temptation

Starter

20 MINS

★ Without looking at the material in session 2, recall the last session and each write an account of what you remember in not more than 100 words. Include things that happened within the group, not just the content of the Bible study.

Once everyone has finished, redistribute the accounts so you are reading out someone else's. Then discuss:

⟳ **Do the accounts disagree or contradict each other at all? If so, how?**

⟳ **Are the differences significant? How did they arise?**

⟳ **Do the accounts taken together tell us more about the event than separately?**

⟳ **Do the differences between the accounts tell us more about the writers than about the event? What do they tell us about the writers?**

★ How did you get on with last session's 'On your own'? Share your views on what Luke wanted to emphasize about Jesus.

Bible study

A. "This is my son ..."

25 MINS

★ For a newcomer to the Bible, one of the first surprises is that the same story is told four times. Then that the four gospels differ in some important, as well as some less important, ways. Read through the background material over the page.

Background

Matthew, Mark, and Luke are known as the "synoptic gospels". The word "synoptic" comes from two Greek words meaning "seen together", and is applied to these gospels because they share so much common material that they could almost be seen as different editions of the same book.

Much of Mark, the shortest, seems to be repeated almost word for word in Matthew and Luke. This has fuelled the belief that Mark was the first of the synoptics to be written, followed by Matthew and Luke, both of whom were familiar with Mark's gospel, and used it.

There is a significant amount of material common to Matthew and Luke which did not originate from Mark, however, and this has led to the conclusion that they used another common source, now lost, which is referred to as "Q" (possibly from "Quelle", a German word for source). In addition to Mark and "Q", Matthew and Luke also drew on a multitude of other sources.

The interesting thing about the way Matthew and Luke adapt Mark's material, and the resulting differences that emerge between the synoptic gospels, lies in what the writer is telling his audience, not whether he got it right.

What about John? John knew and draws from the same traditions as the synoptic gospels, but he treats that material rather differently. Unlike the synoptics, in the fourth gospel we have long speeches by Jesus. And whilst John is drawing on some very early traditions about Jesus, the gospel as a whole probably became a written document some time after the synoptics (approximately AD 90).

While John is in a very different kind of style from the synoptics, we shouldn't make too much of this difference. It is still the same sort of document – a call to faith in Jesus. In particular, we shouldn't fall into the trap of defining the synoptics as historical and John as theological.

★ Each of the four gospels is distinctive in approach, style, and focus. It would be odd to have four if they weren't! Sessions 4–7 investigate the distinctives of each gospel in detail. In this session we'll take a more general view of things. When all four gospels cover the same story, how do they differ? What do we gain from having four accounts? We begin with one of the few stories (outside of Holy Week) that is recorded in all four gospels – the baptism of Jesus.

The passages are printed below to make comparisons easier. Choose a different person to read each version. Highlight in coloured pen any details which are common to each version.

9   Not long afterwards Jesus came from Nazareth in the province of Galilee, and was baptized by John in the Jordan. [10]As soon as Jesus came up out of the water, he saw heaven opening and the Spirit coming down on him like a dove. [11]And a voice came from heaven, "You are my own dear Son. I am pleased with you."

Mark 1.9-11

13   At that time Jesus arrived from Galilee and came to John at the Jordan to be baptized by him. [14]But John tried to make him change his mind. "I ought to be baptized by you," John said, "and yet you have come to me!"
15   But Jesus answered him, "Let it be so for now. For in this way we shall do all that God requires." So John agreed.
16   As soon as Jesus was baptized, he came up out of the water. Then heaven was opened to him, and he saw the Spirit of God coming down like a dove and alighting on him. [17]Then a voice said from heaven, "This is my own dear Son, with whom I am pleased."

Matthew 3.13-17

21   After all the people had been baptized, Jesus also was baptized. While he was praying, heaven was opened, [22]and the Holy Spirit came down upon him in bodily form like a dove. And a voice came from heaven, "You are my own dear Son. I am pleased with you."

Luke 3.21-22

29   The next day John saw Jesus coming to him, and said, "There is the Lamb of God, who takes away the sin of the world! [30]This is the one I was talking about when I said, 'A man is coming after me, but he is greater than I am, because he existed before I was born.' [31]I did not know who he would be, but I came baptizing with water in order to make him known to the people of Israel."
32   And John gave this testimony: "I saw the Spirit come down like a dove from heaven and stay on him. [33]I still did not know that he was the one, but God, who sent me to baptize with water, had said to me, 'You will see the Spirit come down and stay on a man; he is the one who baptizes with the Holy Spirit.' [34]I have seen it," said John, "and I tell you that he is the Son of God."

John 1.29-34

★ Before we try out steps 6 and 7, read the following comment which for brevity's sake suggests some answers to steps 1–5 for you.

Comment

❝ Key steps 3/4
This takes place as the curtain-raiser to Jesus' public ministry. Jordan was the very edge of home territory for Jesus, and John's message and manner of dress confirm him as a latter-day Elijah figure.

Key step 1
One of the aims of the gospel writers seems to be showing that Jesus had an obedient and humble start. They wanted to show that Jesus was special, but by starting with simple obedience rather than a block-busting miracle, they put the subsequent signs of power in new context.

Key step 2
For the New Testament church, baptism was the principal rite of passage into Christianity. Jesus was their model in this, as in all things.

Key step 5
The voice uses words familiar to all Jews from Isaiah 42 which is a description of the Lord's servant, the Messiah. ❞

★ Note that the order in which you take the steps is not always that important. Now to step 6 which is:

Step six

Ask what the writer wants to emphasize

Step 6 will be the main tool used in the rest of the sessions. It brings together the observations you will have made from doing steps 1, 2, and 3, in particular. We will usually take it along with step 7:

Step seven

Compare the emphasis of other related passages

Now apply these steps to the baptism stories by discussing:

⇨ **Taken together, what are the four gospel writers emphasizing through this story?**
⇨ **Taking each writer individually, what (if any) is his special emphasis?**

Summarize your conclusions below:

> **Taken together** ....
>
> ....

> **Taken separately**
>
> **Matthew** ....
>
> **Mark** ....
>
> **Luke** ....
>
> **John** ....

B. "If you are the Son of God..."

★ Immediately after Jesus' baptism the synoptics take Jesus out into the desert, presumably the area beyond the Jordan. Read the accounts of Jesus' temptation below.

12 At once the Spirit made him go into the desert, [13]where he stayed forty days, being tempted by Satan. Wild animals were there also, but angels came and helped him.

Mark 1.12-13

1 Jesus returned from the Jordan full of the Holy Spirit and was led by the Spirit into the desert, [2]where he was tempted by the Devil for forty days. In all that time he ate nothing, so that he was hungry when it was over.

3 The Devil said to him, "If you are God's Son, order this stone to turn into bread."

4 But Jesus answered, "The scripture says, 'Man cannot live on bread alone.'"

5 Then the Devil took him up and showed him in a second all the kingdoms of the world. [6]"I will give you all this power and all this wealth," the Devil told him. "It has all been handed over to me, and I can give it to anyone I choose. [7]All this will be yours, then, if you worship me."

8 Jesus answered, "The scripture says, 'Worship the Lord your God and serve only him!'"

9 Then the Devil took him to Jerusalem and set him on the highest point of the Temple, and said to him, "If you are God's Son, throw yourself down from here. [10]For the scripture says, 'God will order

his angels to take good care of you.' [11]It also says, 'They will hold you up with their hands so that not even your feet will be hurt on the stones.'"

12 But Jesus answered, "The scripture says, 'Do not put the Lord your God to the test.'"

13 When the Devil finished tempting Jesus in every way, he left him for a while.

Luke 4.1-13

1 Then the Spirit led Jesus into the desert to be tempted by the Devil. [2]After spending forty days and nights without food, Jesus was hungry. [3]Then the Devil came to him and said, "If you are God's Son, order these stones to turn into bread."

4 But Jesus answered, "The scripture says, 'Man cannot live on bread alone, but needs every word that God speaks.'"

5 Then the Devil took Jesus to Jerusalem, the Holy City, set him on the highest point of the Temple, [6]and said to him, "If you are God's Son, throw yourself down, for the scripture says,

'God will give orders to his angels about you;
    they will hold you up with their hands,
so that not even your feet will be hurt on the stones.'"

7 Jesus answered, "But the scripture also says, 'Do not put the Lord your God to the test.'"

8 Then the Devil took Jesus to a very high mountain and showed him all the kingdoms of the world in all their greatness. [9]"All this I will give you," the Devil said, "if you kneel down and worship me."

10 Then Jesus answered, "Go away, Satan! The scripture says, 'Worship the Lord your God and serve only him!'"

11 Then the Devil left Jesus; and angels came and helped him.

Matthew 4.1-11

Focus on steps 5, 6, and 7 by discussing:

⇨ **Did any Old Testament characters go through similar experiences to this?**

⇨ **Taken together, what are the writers emphasizing?**

⇨ **Taken separately, do the writers have any special emphasis?**

★ Finally, apply steps 8 and 9, which will be introduced in more detail in the next session.

Step 8 – question the text in the light of your own situation, and your own situation in the light of the text; step 9 – act on your conclusions.

★ What does step 8 suggest for you? Taking the baptism and temptation narratives together – for they are really part of the same story – does this passage have anything to teach you in particular?

★ Are there some principles here? Let's think about how we cope with our "mountain-top" and "desert" experiences. Many people experience aspects of the baptism and temptation story in different ways. Read the following account.

> Brian was terrified of his forthcoming duty as best man, and particularly of having to make his speech. Nevertheless he prayed and put his faith in God, and on the big day he was amazed at how calmly he was able to perform all his duties – he even had the guests in hysterics with his wit and funny stories of the groom. This all left him on a high through the following day, but later in the week he found he was very unsure of himself in a much less daunting situation and consequently felt quite depressed.

> **Have you had experiences similar to this?**
> **Do you find that when God has been very apparent in your life it is sometimes followed by a real testing time?**
> **Looking at Jesus in the temptation passage, how can we draw strength at such times?**
> **What do you learn from this kind of experience?**

★ We are probably all aware of the story of Elijah and the prophets of Baal in 1 Kings 18, but we may be less familiar with the events immediately following it in chapter 19. If you have time, read it and compare it with the story of Jesus' baptism and temptation.

★ Finally, look again at the cards you wrote at the end of session 1 (page 14), and do a progress check at the end of this first unit. Are any of the situations you described for yourself or your church being addressed by these passages or any of the other passages we have covered so far? Write a new card recording your current thoughts.

On your own

★ To prepare for the next session's Starter, think of any three stories, incidents, or anecdotes relating to your own family which you would be happy to share with the group.

4

According To Mark

Aims

- To see how Mark's gospel presents Jesus
- To see how gospel "narrative" speaks to us today
- To investigate the miracles of Jesus

Starter

15 MINS

★ In pairs, share a little of your family history. Tell your partner some family stories, anecdotes, or incidents which you remember concerning your parents, your grandparents, or any generation of the past. Record the main details of your story on the chart below.

Who appears in the story	What happens	Why it is a memorable story in your family
....	....	....
....	....	....
....	....	....
....	....	....

As a group, discuss:

⊳ **What makes a family story worth remembering?**
⊳ **In what contexts are they repeated?**
⊳ **Why are these stories of value in your family?**

Bible study

20 MINS

A. "The right time has come"

★ Sessions 1–3 looked at the gospels as a whole, concentrating on what unites them. Sessions 4–7 will look at each separately, starting here with Mark.

Background

Mark's gospel is shorter than any of the others, and partly for that reason was never too popular in the early church. But in modern times, with the discovery that it was probably the first gospel to be written, Mark has found a new importance.

As a book, it is not a very polished production. Mark's Greek is the sort of colloquial language most of us would associate with the tabloid press in Britain today. But for all its literary weaknesses it is a compelling story, told with great gusto. It has many touches of detail which suggest it was based on the recollections of people who had actually been there. Some early Christians believed it contained the reminiscences of Peter himself, written down by Mark.

It is possible that Mark's fast-moving story was written down in Rome in the mid to late AD 60s. The way he presents Jesus reflects life at the heart of the Roman empire. In Rome, stories of the gods' doings were two a penny and Mark highlights the actions of Jesus more than his words, moving rapidly from one story to the next to show that Jesus' life was really something special.

Jesus' teaching in Mark reflects the concerns of Christians in a city like Rome. How could they cope with persecution when it came? What could they really believe about Jesus – was he a man, or God, or both?

★ Mark depicts Jesus as a great hero – a person of authority, who acts to change situations in a decisive and positive way. Mark's pace is quite breathtaking. Event follows event, with little space given over to inter- pretation or reflection.

A study of Mark's gospel is therefore an appropriate context in which to investigate how we learn from "narrative" in the gospels. This takes us back to step 6.

⇨ Ask what the writer wants to emphasize

★ You should quickly be becoming aware of the diverse types of writing the gospels contain and while the nine steps are always useful to unlock meaning, each type of writing does require a slightly different approach.

We will be concentrating in these next sessions particularly on
1. Stories
2. Teaching
3. Comment

because these are the most common.

★ We begin with stories and how we learn from gospel "narrative" or stories.

Think back to the family stories that you recalled in the starter. Look again at the chart that summarized their significance. Why were your stories worth remembering and retelling? How many of the following were represented?

1. Stories that summed up something about someone's character or attitudes.
2. Stories that warned of stupid behaviour to avoid, or model behaviour to be copied.
3. Stories which were important simply because they changed the course of your family's life.
4. Stories which show God active in your family.
5. Stories which help explain why your family does things the way they do them now.

Were there other categories as well, which are not on this list? If so, list them, and think of some stories which illustrate them.

★ Read together Mark 1.14–2.17, the very first incidents in Jesus' public ministry in Galilee. As a group of passages we could call them "The first miracles and the first disciples".

There are seven individual sections. Take one section each (Mark 1.14-20, 21-28, 29-34, 35-39, 40-45, 2.1-12, 13-17). Quickly summarize it for the rest of the group. Together decide whether these passages individually or collectively include any of the same, or similar, reasons why stories are remembered in your family.

Then, taking the incidents separately, consider step 6.

➢ What does Mark want to emphasize?

Summarize the answer for each passage in a snappy sentence, written on a piece of card. Taking all the passages together, try to summarize in a single slogan or a few key words what Mark was emphasizing in these early narratives. Write the summary slogan in the centre of a large poster-size piece of paper. Stick the rest of the cards around the outside.

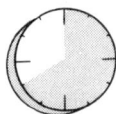

B. Who is this man?

40 MINS

★ In many ways the miracles are the gospel "stories" that cause modern readers most problems, or raise the most difficult questions. We are going to look at some of these questions. Did they really happen that way? Or is there another more "naturalistic" explanation? And if they did happen that way, are we supposed to expect them to happen that way now? Should we be searching for miracles like Jesus' first followers did?

We are shortly going to read together Mark 4.35–5.20, two linked miracle stories.

★ As background to the passage read the comment opposite, which takes you through steps 1–5.

Comment

❝ With these passages we've moved well on into Jesus' public ministry in Galilee (step 3). Mark's story of this phase of Jesus' life is predominantly taken up with miracles. The miracles were part of Mark's proof that Jesus was special (step 1). The Old Testament prophets such as Elijah had set a miracle-working precedent for those that came after (step 5), and the first Christians, particularly those with a Jewish background, would probably expect even more from the Messiah (step 2).

We are still in Galilee, but Jesus is no longer just a local phenomenon. Wherever he goes he causes a stir. His fame has spread throughout the area – but remember the size of the area, around 30 kms across, the size of a small English county (step 4). ❞

★ Read the passages dramatically, and if someone would like to volunteer to add sound effects it will add to the atmosphere. You will need Mark the narrator, Jesus, and The man with the evil spirit. The rest of you read the part of Disciples, and Spirits (verse 11).

Background

Read the following with reference to step 4.

Whether it was Gerasa or Gadara, this story takes place on the pagan territory of Decapolis, hence the herd of pigs which Jews regarded as unclean.

A Roman Legion had its headquarters in Gerasa, and the symbol on their standard was a pig!

▷ **What impact do these stories make on you?**
▷ **Do you find them easy to believe or not?**

★ Now try out step 6, and look for what Mark wants to emphasize. In particular, how does Mark record the impact on the people involved in the original story?

For example, what was the impact on:

■ The disciples
■ The man with the evil spirit
■ The men who had been taking care of the pigs
■ People from the area who were told about it

☞ **Are there any aspects of the story that you think Mark is particularly wanting to draw to his audience's attention?**

★ Now carry out step 8, and reconsider the impact of the stories on you.

★ What is the point of the miracle stories? For a different insight into the place of miracles in Jesus' ministry, we can look outside Mark's gospel. Read Luke 7.18-23.

☞ **What exactly was John asking Jesus here? Express his question in another way.**

☞ **What did Jesus seem to suggest was the point of the miracles?**

In the light of your answers, read Mark 8.11-13. Right at the beginning and right at the end of his ministry Jesus was tempted/taunted to perform a miracle to prove who he was. Read Matthew 4.1-11 and Matthew 27.39-43. Why do you think he refused?

★ Read through the following comment, then discuss:

☞ **Have you ever witnessed a miracle or been convinced of miracles happening to other people?**

☞ **Do you think we can expect Jesus to work such miracles today? How?**

Comment

❝ What is a miracle? There is probably no one answer that satisfies everybody. Some might say that a miracle is anything that goes against the laws of nature. But others may point out that there are no such things as fixed laws of nature – such laws are only rationalizations of our normal experiences of things. Someone in a primitive tribe might see an invention such as the television for the first time and regard it as a miracle – another person will know how it works, and describe it differently. A mother with a long history of miscarriages and still-births has a healthy baby and regards it as a miracle. Someone else can point to the statistics and say it was bound to happen sooner or later.

Yet however people approach the miracles in the gospels, it is clear that they highlight truths about Jesus. They tell of God's intervention in this world and in people's lives; they show a variety of response to Jesus; they tell of God's love and power.

As the Jews expected miracles to be a sign of the Messiah, the miracles recorded in the gospels also emphasize who they believe Jesus to be. **❞**

C. Go and tell your family

★ One of the most valuable functions of stories is that they help us talk about our own situation, particularly where it is similar to that of the story. Therapists mention how much easier clients find it to talk about their own problems if someone is going through a parallel experience in a television soap opera at the time. That's also a valuable function of gospel stories.

So, finally, to the concluding steps 8 and 9. Step 9 follows naturally from step 8.

Step eight

> **Question the text in the light of your own situation and your own situation in the light of the text**

Step nine

> **Act on your conclusions**

Jesus told the man in Mark 5.19, "Go back home to your family and tell them how much the Lord has done for you . . ."

▷ **How well would you cope with this demand?**
▷ **Why is it often most difficult to share our faith with people whom we know (and love) the best?**

★ Are there other things you are experiencing at the moment that are similar to those of the characters in any of the passages you have just looked at?

On your own

★ Sometime before the next session read through Mark's account of the Transfiguration (Mark 9.2-13), which is one of the pivotal stories of the whole gospel.

If we accept the link between Peter and the writer of Mark, this story offers one of the most poignant insights into how Peter felt about the events he relates. There is something quite ridiculous about his "tent" suggestion – a spur of the moment "Peterism" – possibly followed, as verse 6 suggests, by an embarrassed silence.

The story mixes the sublime with the every day in a way no other story in Mark quite seems to.

Concentrate on step 6 – what does the writer want to emphasize? Try out step 5 as well, as Old Testament imagery is an important element of this story.

5

According to Matthew

Aims

- ■ To see how Matthew presents Jesus
- ■ To identify steps for applying Jesus' teaching
- ■ To examine some major themes of Jesus' teaching

Starter

15 MINS

★ Now for the chance you've all be waiting for – to reminisce about your school-days! Break up into smaller groups – three or four to a group, and each briefly describe your best teacher. Who was he/she? What did they teach? How did they teach it? What made them good teachers?

Together as a group again, discuss:

⇨ **What makes a good teacher?**

⇨ **Which of those attributes have you seen in Jesus through your reading of the gospels so far?**

From the following list of techniques, strategies, and styles, and any more you can think of, identify those that Jesus used to get his message across. We'll use the list later, so you will need to save it.

Jesus taught:		
by example	on the move	using notes
by rote	in the course of	off the cuff
from a book	everyday life	in monologue
using parables	with lecture style	in dialogue
using riddles	with preaching style	in group debate
using hyperbole	with three-point	to ordinary people
using visual aids	sermons	to intellectuals
using gimmicks	to a few	appealing to the
apologetically	to many	heart
authoritatively	one to one	appealing to the
persuasively	using mnemonics	head
in buildings	using rhyme	

Bible study

A. You have heard . . . but now I tell you

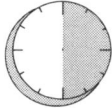

30 MINS

★ Jesus didn't reserve his teaching for the synagogue. To that extent he was a typical Jewish rabbi. He taught on the move, through life events, and at all times. It isn't such a surprise that crowds immediately gathered to listen to Jesus wherever he was. That was what you did when there was a rabbi around! In a time and in a country without mass education (which we take so much for granted now) there wasn't a dividing line between learning and living. Learning happened in the everyday things of life when you were out fishing, eating lunch, or pulling water from a well.

How can we learn from Jesus' teaching? As the background material below makes clear, Matthew's gospel is a good place to find an answer.

Background

Matthew's gospel was for a long time the Church's "favourite" gospel. It contains one of the fullest accounts of Jesus' life and teaching. It includes nearly all the contents of Mark, though re-edited. Because Matthew arranges everything by topic, it is easy to use as a resource for Christian teaching.

One of Matthew's key concerns is to show that in the coming of Jesus, the promises God gave to Israel in the Old Testament had all come true. As we saw in session 2, Old Testament texts are extensively quoted – about 130 direct or indirect references can be identified.

It seems almost certain that Matthew was written for readers with a Jewish background – in fact many commentators have narrowed it down further and suggested that this gospel was written sometime after AD 80 for Christians living in northern Palestine. If that's true, it helps to explain another of Matthew's characteristics – his attitude to Judaism and particularly his record of Jesus' strident criticism of the Pharisees (chapter 23 for instance).

Judaism had only a short time earlier officially outlawed Christianity, and the Christians of northern Palestine were in day to day contact with the Jews of this vigorously anti-Christian Pharisaical tradition. Matthew wants his readers to see the blindness of the Jewish leaders. They waited for a Messiah . . . then missed him when he came. Matthew indicates that the Christians are the true inheritors of the Old Testament promise.

This re-echoes throughout Matthew's record of Jesus' teaching. He organizes it into five sections (each rounded off with the formula "When Jesus finished saying these things . . .")

■ Chapters 5–7, the sermon on the mount which concerns the character, duties, privileges, and destiny of the followers of Jesus.

- Chapters 10–11.1, instructions to the twelve disciples for their mission.
- Chapter 13, parables about the Kingdom of heaven.
- Chapter 18, teaching on the meaning of discipleship.
- Chapters 24–25, teaching about the end of the present age and the coming of the Kingdom of heaven.

★ In the sermon on the mount Jesus turns his attention to a set of questions that would have been very topical for the first-century Christians reading Matthew's gospel. We can't look at them all, but let's focus on three.

Split into three groups, each group taking one of the following passages:

- Matthew 5.17-48
- Matthew 6.1-18
- Matthew 6.19-21, 24-34

Try out steps 2 and 5 to start with. The other steps have been generally covered in the background material above. Then consider step 6 – what does the writer want to emphasize?

The best way to do this is to summarize the teaching in your own words. In the case of many teaching passages this may well be a simple matter. Jesus provides his own summaries, or the author provides one instead.

In the Matthew 5 passage above Jesus provides a formula which can form a basis for summary. Having opened in chapter 5.17 with a general affirmation of all that his hearers would know from the Law of Moses, he then proceeds step by step to challenge some of the pharisaical instructions that had built up over the Law with the formula, "you have heard it said . . . but I say . . ."

Summarize below the teaching of your passage.

....

....

....

★ Coming together again, each group share your summary.

★ Now in your three groups again, try step 7. Look at the first passage from Matthew 5, particularly verses 17-20, where Jesus talks about the Law of Moses. Compare this with the emphasis of other related Bible passages. Each group may like to take one each of the passages suggested below, or find your own passages using a topical concordance or topical listing from a good study Bible.

- Deuteronomy 5–6
- Psalm 119 (as much as you can)
- Galatians 3

Come back together as a group, and briefly summarize what you have discovered. Now look at step 8, which brings together the text and our own situation.

You will already have begun to do this, but we need an intermediate step if we are going to get the "application" right – to identify the audience.

Was Jesus teaching only his close followers – as he did in Matthew 10, for example? Or was this teaching "broadcast" – apparently addressed to whoever wished to listen? The question is worth asking, even if the answer is sometimes "We don't know", because the gospel writers often thought it important to mention who Jesus was addressing. Decide for yourself concerning the sermon on the mount by looking at Matthew 4.25, 5.1-2, and 7.28-29. Then, if you need to, compare your thoughts with our comment.

Comment

" Matthew places this teaching early on in Jesus' public ministry in Galilee. Jesus is pictured on a hillside, disciples around him, addressing a large crowd – Matthew 4.25 suggesting they came from all over Palestine. Certainly Matthew gives a more diverse audience than Mark mentioned in his version of Jesus' public ministry in Galilee. The implication is that this is teaching for everyone – all society even – not just for the inner band of followers. **"**

★ "Pharisaism" has entered our language as an implied criticism. But surely Jesus would not want us to sit back in self-righteousness. What Pharisaical attitudes would he challenge in us? Cast your mind over your own life, individually or as a group, and "criticize" yourself in the light of the passage you summarized on the previous page. Consider how your life or attitudes might better match the requirements of Jesus.

★ Now think briefly about step 9 – how can you act on your conclusions?

B. The Kingdom of heaven is like ...

★ We haven't so far touched on what many would regard as Jesus' most distinctive teaching device – the parables. We will return to them in session 8, particularly those that deal with the Kingdom of God. The word "parable" is related to the two Greek words that mean "to lay one thing alongside another", for the purpose of comparing the two. Jesus often takes everyday situations, sometimes adding a bizarre or unexpected

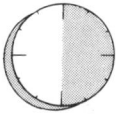

30 MINS

twist, and uses them as illustrations of his message. Their apparent simplicity is deceptive and Jesus used them often not so much to explain things, but to undermine completely common suppositions.

Let's look at some characteristic concerns of parables. Flip through your Bibles and look at the section headings – if you've got a *Good News Bible*, the index at the back lists all the parables. Find at least one parable that appears to deal with:

■ Prayer
■ God's character
■ Humility
■ Forgiveness
■ Being prepared for the Kingdom

Then add to the list any other characteristic themes of parables you can identify.

★ Now split into two groups. Each group choose one subject from your extended list and create a modern parable on that subject, to express what you feel to be Jesus' teaching on this matter. Your parable can be written, spoken, acted, drawn – whatever you like.

When you've formulated the essentials of your parable, present it – albeit in draft form – to the rest of the group.

If you have time, look again at the list of Jesus' teaching strategies from the Starter on page 34. Decide whether your presentations can be improved by considering any other teaching strategies, which would add impact to your parable.

On your own

★ What did Jesus teach his disciples in private? How did his message then differ from the public teaching of the sermon on the mount?

Sometime before the next session, read Matthew 10.5–42. Try out steps 1, 2, and 6.

When you come to step 6, as part of your preparation for the next session, attempt to distill this teaching into a set – about seven – of instructions to the disciples.

Note any of these instructions which deal with the importance of relationships for the disciples as they go out on their mission.

6 According to Luke

Aims

■ To see how Luke presents Jesus

■ To look at Jesus on the road from Galilee to Jerusalem

■ To see what we can learn from Jesus' relationships and attitudes to the people around him

Starter

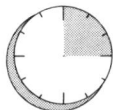

15 MINS

★ As you arrive, write your answers to last session's On your own – the instructions to do with relationships – on the chart provided.

★ Now split into smaller groups. Tell the others about any occasion when you felt left out. Describe the event, how you felt at the time, and your feelings about it now.

Bible study

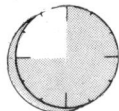

45 MINS

A. Who is my neighbour?

★ Luke's gospel particularly portrays Jesus as a friend and supporter of those whom no one else wanted. Women, tax-collectors, prostitutes, foreigners – all these and other outcasts feature more prominently in Luke than in any other gospel. Unlike the other synoptics he describes Jesus' mission as bringing "Good News to the poor", and this is illustrated in some of Jesus' most distinctive parables. See the parable of the good Samaritan (Luke 10.25–37), for example.

Background

Let's look at step 4. The relationship between Jews and Samaritans in first century Palestine is possibly best compared to that between the two communities in Northern Ireland today where historical factors, as much as religious differences, separate the two.

39

★ There is a risk when you are confronted with a story as familiar as this that you don't really listen, so to encourage everyone to take a close look, the following version has missed out some of the crucial words. Someone volunteer to read it out, filling in the gaps, with the others helping as you go along.

The parable of the good Samaritan

A teacher of the _____ came up and tried to _____ Jesus. " _____ ," he asked, "what must I do to receive _____ ?"

Jesus answered him, "What do the _____ say? How do you interpret them?"

The man answered, "' _____ the Lord your God with all your heart, with all your soul, with all your strength, and with all your mind'; and ' _____ your neighbour as you _____ '".

"You are right," Jesus replied; " _____ and you will live."

But the teacher of the Law wanted to _____ himself, so he asked Jesus, "Who is my _____ ?"

Jesus answered, "There was once a man who was going down from _____ to _____ when robbers attacked him, stripped him, and beat him up, leaving him half dead. It so happened that a _____ was going down that road; but when he saw the man, he _____ on by, on the other side. In the same way a _____ also came along, went over and looked at the man, and then walked on by, on the other side. But a _____ who was travelling that way came upon the man, and when he saw him, his _____ was filled with _____ . He went over to him, poured oil and wine on his wounds and bandaged them; then he put the man on his own _____ and took him to an inn, where he took _____ of him. The next day he took out two silver coins and gave them to the innkeeper. 'Take _____ of him,' he told the innkeeper, 'and when I come back this way, I will _____ you whatever else you _____ on him.'"

And Jesus concluded, "In your _____ , which one of these three acted like a _____ towards the man attacked by the robbers?"

The teacher of the Law answered, "The one who was _____ to him."

Jesus replied, "You go, then, and do _____ ."

Luke 10.25-37

★ Try out step 6, which on this occasion will not cause many problems. The parable seems so simple and immediate.

Now go back to the earlier steps, and see if they might add any extra layers of meaning to the story. Try them out – particularly steps 2, 4, and 5.

Background

Luke is the longest of the gospels. In many ways it seems the most modern, because while it is clearly theological, as are all the gospels, it also appears at various times to be carefully historical, even sociological or psychological – the kind of areas that we expect to hear about today. Luke was probably an educated Greek, and immersed in the analytical way of thinking that the Greeks bequeathed to us.

Luke attempted to make up in research what he lacked in personal experience, and one of his sources was almost certainly Mark's gospel. But it is not certain when he wrote his gospel and it could have been any time between AD 65 and 80.

Luke was probably a doctor, and quite well off. He wrote his gospel for Theophilus – who has been variously interpreted as a real and influential Roman or as a symbolic figure (Theophilus means "lover of God"). As a follow up to his gospel he wrote the book of Acts which covers the spread of Christianity in the years immediately after Jesus' death.

Luke was possibly a companion to Paul who took the gospel to many parts of the known world, and so it is no surprise that Luke majors on the fact that Jesus' message is for everyone. Throughout the gospel, Jesus is always depicted as giving priority to the outcasts of society. More than the other gospel writers, he shows Jesus with a strong social conscience.

He also underlines, however, the importance of spiritual values in Jesus' teaching, focusing on what prayer is about, how to "depend" on the Holy Spirit, and what salvation means.

B. The Kingdom of God belongs to such as these ...

★ Let's see how Luke's emphasis comes out, in a series of incidents drawn from the penultimate phase of Jesus' ministry. He is now on the road from Galilee to Jerusalem. Each of the synoptics puts the turning point shortly after Simon Peter's declaration that Jesus is the Messiah. From that point Jesus begins to talk overtly about his death. Quickly read how Luke introduces this new phase, in Luke 9.51.

★ We will examine four related incidents. Three of these are grouped together in all three synoptics. One is unique to Luke.
Read together Luke 18.15–17, 18.18–29, 18.35–43, and 19.1–9.
Let's concentrate on step 6. What does the writer want to emphasize? In particular:

    ➳ **How was Jesus' behaviour unusual or unexpected to those around him?**
    ➳ **How did they express their disapproval?**
    ➳ **What does Luke show was the impact of the interaction on the rich man, the blind beggar, or on Zacchaeus?**

41

★ Before reading the following comment, try to summarize what overall emphasis we get from these Lucan stories about Jesus' attitudes. How did these attitudes differ from those around him?

Comment

ሬሬ We have some unlearning to do if we are really to appreciate Luke's emphasis. We have for so long been reading about *good* Samaritans, *reformed* tax collectors, and *healed* invalids, that we forget that what Jesus did in according status to such people was as unexpected as it was radical. Even the little children pose us a problem, because childhood is romanticized and worshipped in many of our churches.

So to summarize: Jews had no dealings with Samaritans; they did not think religion had any place for children, they thought wealth was a sign of God's blessing, and therefore a sign of God's acceptance. They thought that physical suffering (such as blindness) was a sure sign of God's displeasure, and they hated tax collectors as only Roman stooges could be hated.

Jesus came in and turned everything upside down. **ፃፃ**

★ Now try out the following activity, which will help you apply Luke's emphasis as a whole to your situation today (step 8).

■ Through discussion, identify for yourselves who in today's society is the equivalent of the Samaritans, the children, the poor, the blind, and the tax collector.

■ Then decide who is the equivalent of the rich man, the Pharisee, and the rulers.

On the chart opposite, write under the heading "Groups/individuals", your answers to the above questions. Now on the top line grade yourself as to how high a priority you give to these people groups. On the bottom line grade your church.

Personal and church assessment sheet

Groups/individuals	Low priority					High priority
1.	**Self**	1	2	3	4	5
	Church	1	2	3	4	5
2.	**Self**	1	2	3	4	5
	Church	1	2	3	4	5
3.	**Self**	1	2	3	4	5
	Church	1	2	3	4	5
4.	**Self**	1	2	3	4	5
	Church	1	2	3	4	5
5.	**Self**	1	2	3	4	5
	Church	1	2	3	4	5
6.	**Self**	1	2	3	4	5
	Church	1	2	3	4	5
7.	**Self**	1	2	3	4	5
	Church	1	2	3	4	5
8.	**Self**	1	2	3	4	5
	Church	1	2	3	4	5
9.	**Self**	1	2	3	4	5
	Church	1	2	3	4	5
10.	**Self**	1	2	3	4	5
	Church	1	2	3	4	5

⊐➔ **Does this chart highlight any areas in which you would like to make changes?**

⊐➔ **What could you do as an individual or group to implement these changes?**

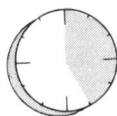

C. Into Jerusalem

25 MINS

★ Now we come into the period of Jesus' life which is covered in great detail by all the gospel writers, and usually in much the same order.

Read Luke 19.28-48, and compare it with Matthew's version of events in Matthew 21.1-17.

★ Can you find evidence of Luke's characteristic emphasis on Jesus' concern for the outsider in the account of Jesus driving the money-lenders from the Temple?

You probably found the reverse is the case. This can be a warning to us not to fall into the trap of over emphasizing the distinct perspective of each gospel writer. Yes, Luke does bring out Jesus' concern for the underdog more clearly but this facet of Jesus is present in the other gospel writers, too. Likewise, Matthew doesn't have a monopoly on Jesus' teaching!

★ For the final part of this session, let's look again at Luke's emphasis on the way Jesus related to the outsiders of society. In some ways rich, educated, cosmopolitan Luke is the most unlikely champion of the poor, the outcasts, and the rejects.

As a man in a very male world, he is also an unlikely champion of women. Yet Luke is characteristically concerned with the role of women in Jesus' ministry. Luke shows that Jesus is clearly in touch with the needs of the women he meets. He is also the only gospel writer who devotes a special section to listing the women who went with Jesus on his travels through Galilee (Luke 8.1-3).

Turn back to that passage, and the moving story which precedes it (Luke 7.36-50). Read the story, and then to find out what Luke is emphasizing, discuss:

☞ **What is the woman offering Jesus? What does Jesus offer the woman? Try to look beyond the obvious.**

☞ **What does Luke show was the effect of this transaction on her and on others who observed it?**

Comment

❝ Jesus' real gift to the outsider was acceptance and forgiveness. So was Jesus really such a radical as we seem to be suggesting? Maybe.

Like us, and like the New Testament church itself, Jesus was caught in the tension of wanting to help individuals and individual sin, yet challenge ingrained prejudice and injustice in society – or what some call 'structural sin'. Luke catches this tension. Jesus, according to Luke, helps change the society around him, starting with individuals. Yet at the same time he engages in a sustained battle with the establishment. Luke's gospel encourages us, therefore, to avoid easy prescriptions for change. We will return to this theme in session 8, on the Kingdom of God.

The ultimate sign that Jesus' mission was not political in the 'government' sense is that Jesus doesn't challenge the Romans, as so many of his followers would have liked him to do. Instead, it was political in the personal sense. In Jesus' eyes, everybody was given the power to become a child of God. **"**

On your own

★ Before the next session, go out on a bit of local research.

The traditions of the medieval church assigned a symbolic animal or image to each of the gospel writers or "evangelists".

These were based upon:

- Matthew as the winged man
- Mark as the (winged) lion
- Luke as the (winged) ox
- John as the eagle.

Medieval churches, and even some very modern ones, have incorporated this symbolism into their furnishings and fabric. See if you can spot any of them. Note in particular where the symbols appear.

7

According to John

Aims

- To see how John presents Jesus
- To identify and learn from the theological comment within gospel writing
- To explore the story of the Last Supper

Starter

15 MINS

★ How did you get on with last session's On your own? Share your findings. In particular, where did you find John's eagle?

★ Your leader will read out extracts from four versions of a very famous story which appears in all four gospels. Without referring to your Bibles, try to identify John's version from the synoptics. If you are really clever you may be able to sort out the synoptics, as well. Record your ideas below.

> 1. ....
> 2. ....
> 3. ....
> 4. ....

⇨ **Did you get it right? How did you identify John's version?**

Bible study

25 MINS

A. Jesus the bread of life

★ Every writer has a style. John's gospel is more reflective than the three synoptics. This is obvious even from the opening paragraphs of the book. Look quickly at John 1.1–5 (you'll be returning to this "prologue" later).

John is very clearly drawing from the same tradition as the synoptics, but his story flows in a slower, more dignified, fashion than the others. It gives the impression of being a thoughtful meditation on the meaning of Jesus. Jesus' teachings in John are recorded not in the form of short-story parables but in longer and more theological talks to his disciples. Often it seems that John has included in his gospel only those stories which lend themselves to extended commentary.

John's gospel is therefore the ideal context in which to investigate the particular problems associated with understanding "comment" in the gospels. Read together one of these theological commentaries, John 6.25-59, a direct sequel to the feeding of the five thousand. John writes it as a dialogue between Jesus and the people, so read it in that way. You'll need one person as John the narrator; another to read Jesus; the rest of you read the crowd – grumbles and all.

As in previous sessions, we are going to focus our study on step 6 – what does the writer want to emphasize? But as there's so much going on in the story, let's untangle it a bit to start with. Break into three groups, and each consider one of the following:

⇨ **Where does the dialogue appear to have taken place? (verses 25 and 59)**

⇨ **What is the main point that Jesus is making?**

⇨ **What seems to be the main objection of the people to what he's saying?**

★ Come back together and read the following comment, which runs through the earlier steps.

Comment

❝ Let's look at step 4. Jesus was a teacher, and we would expect him to teach his disciples in the style of a rabbi, the religious teacher of his day. A rabbi would pick out a piece of teaching from the past – often a story or a saying found in the Old Testament – and interpret it for the present. He would give his discourse or 'Midrash' as he and his disciples were on the move, or in a synagogue.

This passage has taken us back to an earlier phase in Jesus'· public ministry in Galilee (step 3). In this case the 'feeding' miracle has reminded the people of the 'manna' miracle of the Old Testament – you can read it in Exodus 16 (step 5). John presents Jesus in rabbinic fashion, explaining the significance of both miracles. Although John's Jesus may speak in the style of a rabbi, however, he says things no other rabbi would dare.

The people don't seem to be getting the point, and what worries them most is that Jesus, son of Joseph and Mary, an ordinary person, is making claims about himself. He is the bread of life; he has come down from heaven; he offers eternal life. ❞

★ Now discuss step 6 – what does John want to emphasize?

Discuss your own ideas as a group. Is John most interested in what Jesus has to say, in how the people reacted, in both of these, or in something else altogether? Discuss your ideas.

⇨ **What claims, implicit or explicit, are being made for Jesus in this passage?**

47

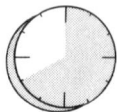

40 MINS

B. The servant king

★ John 6.53-58 makes an implicit link for John's readers into the story of the Last Supper. That is what we'll look at for the second half of this session.

Most Christian churches today practise some form of Eucharist, Communion, or Fellowship meal – a ritual which has actually changed very little over two thousand years. Let's look at what John tells us of this centre-piece of Christian faith.

John's version of the Last Supper takes five whole chapters – almost one-sixth of his gospel.

By flipping through chapters 13–17 looking just at the headings, try to answer:

> ▷ **What two incidents does John's account have in common with the other three gospels?**
> ▷ **What key incident told in the other three gospels is not present in John's account of the Last Supper?**

★ John's account of the Last Supper is really an extended meditation on the nature of discipleship. Run through steps 1–5, applying them to the Last Supper narrative as a whole. By now you will have realized from examples given that there is no need to be too systematic about these steps. Any gaps will be revealed in due course.

For step 6, a number of elements of discipleship have been identified below which seem typical of the narrative as a whole.

1. Serving/caring – 13.1-20
2. Loving – 13.31-35, 15.1-17
3. Believing – 14.1-4
4. Obeying – 14.15-31
5. Standing firm against persecution – 15.18–16.4
6. Receiving the Holy Spirit – 14.15-31, 16.4-15

Choose one or more of these elements so that they are parcelled out between you, and on your own try out step 6 – what is the emphasis? Share your ideas with the rest of the group.

Read John 16.25–17.26, which brings all these points together in a kind of summary prayer.

★ Now try out steps 8 and 9. As a practical focus for action, redesign the Communion service – as it is currently practised in the various churches you attend – according to John's criteria.

What elements need to be added/deleted, or emphases changed, to make the service better reflect what John wanted to emphasize in the story of the Last Supper?

Background

John's prologue gets his story of Jesus off to a very different start from the other gospels. The Greek for "word" is "logos", and in prevailing Greek philosophy it was often identified with the energy that kept the whole world going. In effect John says to his readers, "This view is correct – only you need to remember it is Jesus who is God's Word and the centre of the universe".

Perhaps John's gospel was written to win such people to faith in Jesus. Certainly it had an evangelistic purpose. The other gospels did, too, but in John 20.31 this purpose is made particularly clear. And the way Jewish customs and ideas are carefully explained suggests it was written for a wide range of people with a non-Jewish background (step 1).

But that does not cut it adrift from the roots of Jesus' own lifetime in Palestine. Unlike the synoptics, John presents Jesus in the mainstream of theological debate of the time. Thus much of the action takes place in Jerusalem and Judea from early on in the gospel. Many aspects of its descriptions of people and places show that it was based on reliable knowledge of the land of Jesus' birth. It may be that this gospel has come into being in stages. First, written down on the basis of John the apostle's recollections in Palestine, for readers there; later revised and edited to make it suitable for a wider non-Jewish readership somewhere else in the Roman empire, perhaps Ephesus or Alexandria.

John was probably the last gospel to appear, but it was still written within the second half of the first century AD.

On your own

The Word

★ Words are one of the ways we communicate with one another, and Jesus as God's supreme communication with the world is appropriately called "the Word". The idea does not reappear elsewhere in the gospel, however – it is only in the prologue. Sometime before the next session, read John 1.1-18.

Look at steps 1–5 – the background material above will help you. Then concentrate on step 6.

In particular, what does the writer want to emphasize about:

■ God
■ Jesus
■ People's reactions to God
■ The way God relates to the world and its inhabitants.

Now look at step 8. It will hopefully be obvious by now that as we seek to apply the gospels today we are looking for much more than models of behaviour or teaching to follow. Sometimes, indeed, we may realize the relevance of a passage for us through our feelings. The gospel can act upon our emotions and thoughts, as well as our behaviour. John's prologue can be one such passage, which acts on us from within. To apply it to our lives it may help to balance the more cerebral kind of approaches we have been using so far with an approach involving our emotions as well as our knowledge.

As the passage is essentially poetic, try using a poetic device to respond to it, and particularly to the following elements:

- God's control of creation
- People rejecting God
- The messenger preparing the way for God
- Any other elements that strike you.

Some people are very unsure of themselves in poetry so if you are stuck, try following this way of formulating a poem:

- a noun (preferably a short one)
- an -ing word
- a five-syllable (or more) line describing the noun
- another -ing word
- the same noun

★ Be prepared to display or read your poem at the next session.

8

Past, present, and future

Aims

- To investigate the "trial" of Jesus
- To explore Jesus' teaching about the Kingdom of God
- To identify what part we can play in God's kingdom

Starter

15 MINS

★ As you arrive, look through the cuttings that are provided concerning the British royal family. With a partner, draw up a set of statements that sum up the views they represent concerning the ideal role for members of the royal family, and in particular for the reigning monarch.

Discuss together:

⇨ **What do you think of the royal family and the monarch?**
⇨ **What does the word "queen" and "king" suggest for you?**

Bible study

40 MINS

A. Are you the king of the Jews?

★ Having looked at the distinctive concerns of each of the four gospels (sessions 4–7) we can once more take a broader view in this unit, and see what the gospels have to say, taken together, about the Kingdom of God (this session), and about the meaning of Jesus' life (session 9).

★ When we come to the Bible's teaching on the Kingdom of God we have some unhelpful prejudices about kingship to clear out of the way. Some of your own feelings about royalty will have surfaced in the Starter.

Imagine a non-Christian friend asks you to define just what it is Christians mean by the Kingdom of God. What would you say? After a brief discussion together, make a list of the characteristics you would single out. Now read the following background material.

Background

Jesus' teaching about the Kingdom of God (or the Kingdom of heaven, in Matthew) was related to the expectations of the people he addressed. Being Jews, they naturally thought in Old Testament categories. They remembered David as the ideal king, and although later kings had debased the monarchy, God had promised to restore the Davidic throne

51

and rule in person through a messiah who would be the descendant of David. So although Israel may look like any other kingdom, it would in reality be God's kingdom, and the kings who ruled would be there in God's place, ensuring that the kingdom reflected the values and standards that were important to God.

At least that was the theory. It had not always worked out in practice, largely due to the self interest of most of Israel's kings. By Jesus' day all chance of independent nationhood seemed past, with the coming of the all-powerful Romans. But people were still clinging to the old promises, and hoping for God to do something new. When Jesus arrived with talk of God's kingdom, his message struck just the right chord for many. It was just what they wanted to hear, and that's why people other than Jesus were claiming to announce the arrival of the "Kingdom", too. Many others were claiming that they were God's annointed leader, and they wanted to get rid of the Romans and bring in God's reign, with themselves at the head of it!

The Kingdom of God is a key element of Jesus' teaching in the synoptics. And even in John, where it is not a predominant theme, it is clear that God's kingdom was a subject of crucial concern for Jesus' hearers (John 6.1-15).

★ The Kingdom was certainly a crucial concern for the various players in Jesus' "trial", particularly as recorded by John.

We saw in the last session how one of John's aims (step 1) was to re-interpret Jesus for a wide non-Jewish audience. Many members of the New Testament church had no roots in Judaism (step 2), so talk of the Kingdom of God would not be as immediately suggestive for them as it was for Jesus' original hearers. In fact the situation of John's audience might be a lot closer to ours today, rather mystified by the term "Kingdom". "Are you a king, then?" asks Pilate incredulously.

★ Read John 18.28–19.16. It cries out to be read dramatically – it is, after all, a conversation. You will need John the narrator, Pilate, the Jewish authorities (including chief priests and temple guards), Jesus and soldiers (19.2-3). The rest of you read the crowd.

★ Steps 3 and 4 are going to be quite useful here. Try them out, comparing them with the ideas in the following Comment, if you wish.

Comment

❝ Step 3: We've reached the very climax of the gospel story, and left Galilee far behind. Since arriving in Jerusalem to shouts of 'God bless the king . . .', Jesus has had almost a week in or near the capital city. By his words and his actions he has challenged the wisdom and authority of the Jewish leaders, and they have arrested him. Now they have a problem – what do they do with him?

Step 4: To start with, the setting is the Jewish centre of religious power at the High Priest, Caiaphas', house. With first light the action shifts to the centre of political power at the Roman governor, Pilate's, palace (Luke's version of the story adds another political dimension when Pilate sends Jesus to King Herod). God's plan is being 'put into action', albeit un-wittingly, by the very highest authorities in Jerusalem. **99**

★ It appears that the Jewish authorities are more worried about Jesus than the Roman authorities are. Split into two groups and as a way into step 6, try out the following activity. Pilate has asked you (his personal assistants) to agree a short statement to be sent back to Rome as part of Pilate's weekly report on affairs in the occupied territory of Palestine. The report must cover:

■ Pilate's causes for concern about Jesus. What threat did he pose?
■ Pilate's personal assessment of what Jesus is saying about himself. Use "transcripts" of the words from the trial. What seems to be the point Jesus is making about the Kingdom?
■ Pilate's reasons for taking the action he did.
■ Pilate's personal assessment of Jesus.

★ Get back together, and read out your reports. Then discuss:

➪ **How does your own assessment of Jesus and his teaching about the Kingdom differ from Pilate's?**
➪ **What strikes you most about Jesus' behaviour in this passage?**
➪ **What is John wanting to emphasize in this story?**

Comment

66 The gospel writers saw Jesus' suffering as part of God's plan. Through the story of Jesus' arrest and trial – a night of frenzied activity and dubious legal practice, Jesus' stately pace makes a marked contrast.

By the time John's gospel was complete, the New Testament church faced significant opposition. While official 'state' persecution had not yet begun, the Christians faced pressure of all kinds. John's readers doubtless drew encouragement from Jesus' great strength when faced by verbal, physical, and emotional abuse. **99**

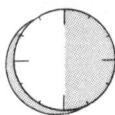

B. "The Kingdom of God is like ..."

30 MINS

★ What is it about Jesus' teaching on the Kingdom that so worried the authorities? Look again at the list of features of the Kingdom that you prepared at the beginning of the session (page 51). Does it look threatening? There are probably things you now want to change or add.

Jesus' teaching about the Kingdom is spread throughout the synoptic gospels. The passages suggested below have been chosen to represent a balance of things Jesus has said about it. You might want to add others.

Share out the passages, one for each person, and read your passage to yourself. Then each person summarize for the group what Jesus is emphasizing about the Kingdom in your passage (step 6). Compare this emphasis with that of the other passages (step 7). Now draw up a new list of characteristics of the Kingdom, incorporating your earlier list and the insights offered by these passages.

■ Matthew 6.24-34
■ Matthew 12.22-32
■ Matthew 25.31-46
■ Matthew 25.1-13
■ Mark 10.13-16

■ Mark 10.35-45
■ Luke 13.18-21
■ Luke 13.22-30
■ Luke 17.20-21
■ John 18.36

Finally, as a way of summarizing:

➢ **Is the Kingdom of God a place, a way of life, a personal attitude or disposition, or something else altogether?**
➢ **What elements of the Kingdom seem to be in the past?**
➢ **What in the present? What in the future?**

Comment

❝ The Kingdom of God is bigger than just the teaching we have about it in the gospels. The idea embraces the gospel writers' view of Old Testament history and it links us back into the Old Testament Law. Through the sayings of Jesus concerned with the future/end times, it also takes us forward into Revelation. The Kingdom of God is 'already, but not yet'. It is a reality that Christians can enjoy now, yet something that they also have to work towards; something that influences even those who don't believe in it. It is both 'eternal life', and earthly rule. It is, in short, a most slippery concept. You think you've caught hold of it, and then realize there's another side to it. **❞**

★ Let's apply step 8 to all we have discovered so far about the Kingdom. Discuss:

> **What responsibilities do you (individually, and as a group) have within this Kingdom of God?**

★ Now apply step 9. Attempt to clarify at least three points of possible action to help you further the influence of God's kingdom in the world today.

On your own

★ Sometime before the next session, do an analysis of your own situation. Examine the practical possibilities for putting into action the points you decided on above.

A matter of life and death

Aims

- To explore the gospels' account of the death and resurrection of Jesus

- To see how the disciples changed as a result of meeting the risen Jesus

- To investigate the impact of Jesus' death and resurrection on the world today

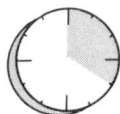

20 MINS

Starter

★ As you arrive, record your conclusions from the last session's On your own, on the chart provided. Note any similarities/distinctives of the action plans.

★ Get into pairs. Life is full of meetings – not only church meetings, but individual encounters, some of which prove to be very significant. Tell the story of some significant meeting in your life – an interview; meeting your boyfriend/girlfriend, husband/wife; meeting a famous person, etc.

Still in pairs, consider:

▷ **Were there any events that preceded this meeting, and added to its significance?**

▷ **How did this meeting change your life afterwards?**

▷ **Did you recognize how significant it would be at the time?**

▷ **What feelings do you now have about this meeting?**

Bible study

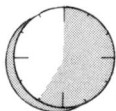

35 MINS

A. It is finished!

★ To close this course we return to where we started, the death and resurrection of Jesus. These events gave meaning to Jesus' life, transformed the first disciples into the bold leaders of the first Christians, and enabled a thriving international church to be built out of a scattered band of Galileans.

Why did Jesus die, and what was the significance of his death according to the gospel writers?

Read the following passages – Matthew 16.21-28; 17.22-23; 20.17-19. Concentrate on step 6, and discuss:

▷ **How did Jesus expect to die?**

▷ **Why did he think it would happen?**

★ Now let's look at John's description of what actually did happen. Someone read John 19.16-42.

As we are dealing with such familiar material, we may have difficulty seeing it in a fresh way. The steps will help us get below the surface of this passage. Run quickly through steps 1–5, comparing with the following comment if you wish.

Comment

❝ The crucifixion lies at the heart of the gospel writers' message (step 1), and the New Testament church's mission (step 2). John's gospel, which began on a high with a 'cosmic' picture of Jesus, now finds Jesus at this very lowest point (step 3), subjected to the most degrading and brutal death the Roman empire had devised. The precise method of crucifixion varied from one part of the empire to another, as did the exact shape of the cross used. Sometimes victims would be tied to it, at other times they would be nailed. This was the method used in Jesus' case, and was probably the usual Palestinian practice, as the skeletons of crucified people discovered there have shown (step 4). In other important ways John sees various aspects of the crucifixion as fulfilling Old Testament prophecy (John 19.24, 28, 36, and 37) (step 5). ❞

★ There are clearly layers of meaning in this story that go beyond the other stories we have studied from the gospels. This, in a way, is "the story". Briefly consider your own view of what John is trying to emphasize (step 6). Now consider the comment below:

Comment

❝ In some Christian traditions the death of Jesus has been seen in symbolic terms. It sets a precedent, or provides a model to follow. In the words of a very famous hymn, Christ's death teaches us 'to suffer and to die'.

In other traditions this event is seen in theological terms. For example, God uses Jesus' death to 'balance the books', and so Jesus dies instead of us. Alternatively, death is necessary before new life is possible.

For the gospel writers this event had an immense emotional impact. Still fresh in their memory – some of them perhaps eyewitnesses of his very gruesome death – they remembered it as any friend would remember the unexpected death of a loved one. ❞

⤳ **Which of these aspects of the story do you think seem uppermost in John's account of the death of Jesus?**

★ Turn back to session 1 and the observation we made then about Matthew's emphasis (page 12). Do you see any contrasts or similarities between John's and Matthew's emphases (step 7)?

Imagine you are one of the disciples, particularly Peter, and how you would have felt immediately following Jesus' death and burial. You are likely to feel a whole range of conflicting emotions, and have many questions in your mind. Try to express these thoughts and feelings by writing five separate words, not a sentence, and share these in the group together.

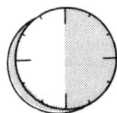

B. Alive again

30 MINS

★ Death is only one side of the gospel coin. What motivated the early Christians as they took their message beyond Palestine and into the main cities of the Roman empire was their conviction that Jesus was not dead, but alive. They preached about his death because they believed he rose again. And they knew this, because they had met him.

Briefly recap in your own mind the significant meeting you remembered in the Starter.

For the final study in this course, we turn to the story of the disciples' meetings with the risen Jesus. Although they might not have known it at the time, no one who met the risen Jesus was ever the same again.

Let's use John's version, which is the most detailed (see Background, opposite), and focus on the moving story of Peter's "rehabilitation" as told in John 21.1-19. It might help you recapture some of the mystery and atmosphere of this night-time fishing trip if you turn the lights down low. One person read verses 1-14, another read verses 15-19.

★ Our first concern is with step 6. What do you think John wants to emphasize? Share your ideas with the rest of the group. Treat verses 1-14 and 15-19 separately for the purpose of this question.

Background

John's gospel deals more fully with the post-resurrection appearances of Jesus than the other gospels (although Luke gives a detailed account of the encounter on the road to Emmaus, which the others don't). John dwells on human details – Peter's robe, the number of fish, the distance to the shore, the charcoal fire. Likewise, his stories ring with the emotional truth of the story. This writer knows how the disciples were feeling.

In contrast, the earliest gospel of them all, Mark, has a rather unusual ending. The story ends with an empty tomb, and the resurrection meetings described in verses 9-20 were not part of the earliest manuscripts. If these were a foundation of the faith of the first Christians, why did Mark's gospel not originally include them? Was the original ending lost perhaps? Or were the first appearances so much a part of the everyday conversation and experiences of the first Christians that Mark didn't even feel the need to set them down?

Matthew's gospel is also very sparing in its coverage of Jesus' appearances to his disciples. Jesus meets the women, and through them gives instructions to the disciples to meet him back on home territory in Galilee, where he instructs them – in the words of the Great Commission – to make disciples everywhere.

★ Now go back to John's story, and for the last time in this book look at steps 8 and 9, the significance of this story for us today.

We'll take as our starting point its significance for Peter. Jesus meets Peter at his point of greatest need, and offers him a new start. It will have been fresh in Peter's mind that he had disowned Jesus under pressure (John 18.15-18, 25-27). He had given up hope, and gone back to his old profession – fishing. What Peter needed more than anything was a chance to renew his relationship with Jesus.

In pairs or threes, think of any aspect of your own situation in which you feel you want to renew your relationship with Jesus. You may, like Peter, have failings or regrets that interfere with your relationship to Jesus. You may have doubts about Jesus. Whatever your situation, if you feel you can share it with the group then do so, and pray together for each other.

★ Now get back together. Your leader will bring out the cards you wrote in session 1 and 3 (pages 14, 27). Remind yourself of what aspects of your own and your church's situations you hoped the gospels would speak to. How far have those hopes been realized? Can you summarize the significance of the gospels for that situation?

★ Finally, use the rest of the session to discuss how you can follow up this series of Bible studies. If you think another Jigsaw book would be useful, there is a list on page 64.

On your own

★ You began this course by defining what a gospel was. Return to your definition (page 10), and reconsider it one last time.

Detailed notes on leading each session

The more your group puts into these studies, the more they'll get out of them. One of the leader's main tasks is to encourage the group, and so to generate interest and enthusiasm about what the gospels have to say to us.

Depending upon the group, a leader would probably need to spend between one and two hours preparing a session. On page 6 are some general notes. These following pages contain more detailed advice.

Session 1

Page 14: For the Application, use small 5 × 3″ record cards – one colour for "personal", another for "church". Keep these cards safe, for use in sessions 3 and 9.

Session 2

There's quite a lot to prepare in this session.

Page 15: Do the starter activity yourself, beforehand. There should be about forty-four movements to map up to the last week in Jerusalem.

Page 18: Paragraph 1. The idea is that you create your own archaeology. You could have: a piece of sheep's wool; a fish bone or two; some grains of wheat, or a bit of straw; anything with some Latin writing on it; a grape; a piece of rock; and a white sheet which could be mistaken for a Roman toga!

Page 18: Paragraph 1. In recording the ideas you may wish to use a spider diagram – i.e. rather than lists, establish a few key ideas, then relate other points to these as they are mentioned. Keep this diagram for reference in future sessions.

Page 19: Paragraph 6. Use a sheet of Filofax or personal organizer paper, for each reference. The following is a list of twenty "OT Fax" references you could use. If you want more – quantity is one of the points to get across – then the footnotes of the *Good News Bible* have them all! Isaiah 7.14, Micah 5.2, Hosea 11.1, Jeremiah 31.15, Deuteronomy 8.3, Psalm 91.11-12, Isaiah 9.1-2, Exodus 20.13, 1 Kings 10.4-7, Hosea 6.6, Malachi 3.1, 1 Samuel 21.1-6, Isaiah 42.1-4, Jonah 1.17, Psalm 78.2, Genesis 2.24, Zechariah 9.9, Jeremiah 7.11, 2 Chronicles 24.20-21, Zechariah 11.12-13.

A concordance will be fairly essential for this activity.

Session 3

Page 21: Paragraph 4. The point of last session's On your own was how the details mirror those of Jesus' death and resurrection.

Session 4

Page 28: Paragraph 2. Picking the right stories is important to the success of this exercise. Lead by example, and tell them your own stories. Make your own stories: a story which sums up something about someone's character; a story which shows some amusing incident; a story which established some precedent for your family.

Page 30: In the feedback, paragraph 4, take notes on a large chart using the categories on page 30 as your basis.

Page 30: Paragraph 4. Two people can do the same section, but still work individually for best results.

Page 30: Paragraph 4. Make a chart which mirrors your earlier one very closely. Use 5 × 3″ record cards.

Session 5

Page 36: Paragraphs 4–5. You could refer back to the list of New Testament concerns from session 1, page 13.

Page 38: Paragraph 2. Make this list a big chart, so that everyone can see what they have to choose from for their parable.

Page 38: Paragraph 3. Put a strict ten-minute time limit on the creation of the parable, otherwise people will go on for hours.

Session 6

Page 39: Paragraph 2. Have a big sheet available for people to write their conclusions on, and fill in one observation of your own at the start.

Page 43: The first column of the chart should be filled in during your discussion – by general agreement.

Page 44: Paragraph 8. The key point here is that Jesus is offering the woman acceptance.

Session 7

Page 46: Paragraph 2. John's eagle is commonly associated with the lectern in Anglican churches – and the lectern is often in the shape of an eagle.

Page 46: Paragraph 3. The four passages for study cover part of the feeding of the five thousand: Matthew 14.14-17, Mark 6.34-38, Luke 9.12-13, John 6.4-9. One of the distinctive "Johnisms" shows itself in the *Good News Bible* in the use of (brackets) for comments by the author. If you feel unable to express this in reading, an alternative is to type the four versions so that there's no indication of which version is which, and photocopy them for each person.

Page 48: Paragraph 4. John has the prediction of Judas' betrayal and the prediction of Peter's denial in common with other gospels. It is the breaking of bread itself which is most conspicuously absent from John's account.

Session 8

Page 51: Paragraph 2. Hopefully this session will coincide with the week of some hot royal news, but the cuttings don't have to be current. For the feedback, use a big sheet of paper for the chart.

Page 54: Paragraph 3. For the feedback chart use four headings: When to expect it; How to recognize it; How it works; How to respond to it.

Session 9

Page 56: Paragraph 2. For the feedback, use a chart with two columns: Action points; Action to be taken.

Summary of the steps for understanding gospels today

Step 1   Identify the aim(s) of the gospel writers

Step 2   Relate the passage to the situation of the New Testament church

Step 3   Identify where this passage fits in the gospel story as a whole

Step 4   Locate the events in first-century Palestine

Step 5   Identify the Old Testament background to the passage

Step 6   Ask what the writer wants to emphasize

Step 7   Compare the emphasis of other related passages

Step 8   Question the text in the light of your own situation, and your own situation in the light of the text

Step 9   Act on your conclusions

Other Jigsaw books

The Jigsaw series helps you understand and piece together the many different kinds of literature you find in the Bible. The six volumes introduce ways of reading and applying Old Testament Law, History, Poetry and Prophets; and New Testament Gospels and Letters.

Each volume has eight or nine easy-to-lead sessions, including key questions which build into a complete methodology for reading each kind of literature.

Titles in the series are:

Understanding Old Testament Law today
by Chris Wright

The books of the Law have the potential to be the most difficult and obscure part of the whole Bible.

In this study Chris Wright has succeeded in making them comprehensible, relevant, and fun. In particular the book highlights the corporate emphasis of much Old Testament Law which has so much to offer us in our present individualistic culture.

Understanding Old Testament History today
by Mike Butterworth

takes you through Israel's history from Joshua to Esther, helping you to discover how valuable and relevant Israel's history can be today. Subjects covered include Joshua and the conquest of Canaan; Israel's golden age under David and Solomon; Ezra, Nehemiah, and the return from exile.

Understanding Poetry and Wisdom today
by John Goldingay

explores the many varied real-life experiences described in the books of Job, Psalms, Proverbs, Ecclesiastes, Song of Songs, and Daniel. Using nine poetry and wisdom checkpoints, the studies explore subjects as varied as worship and lament in the Psalms; views on wealth and sexuality in Proverbs and Song of Songs; understanding suffering with the help of Job.

Understanding Old Testament Prophets today
by Tom Stuckey

plants you firmly in the shoes of the Old Testament prophets from Isaiah to Malachi, and helps you understand their world and listen with new interest to their message, telling what God wishes for his people. Finally, you are challenged to see today's world from the viewpoint of an Old Testament prophet.

Understanding New Testament Letters today
by Tom Stuckey

gives a bird's eye view of the New Testament church in action, taking you behind the letters to see why and how they were written. It allows you to compare your own church with those of the New Testament – often a humbling experience.